Amidst Madness and Hope

Maysie Stott-Morrison

BookLeaf Publishing

India | USA | UK

Cover design by Karen Stott

Presentation by *BookLeaf Publishing*

Web: www.bookleafpub.com

E-mail: info@bookleafpub.com

ISBN: 9789358318333

First edition 2023

DEDICATION

This book is dedicated to my late grandad, David Andrew Stott. His passion for and understanding of words helped me to recognise the same qualities in myself. He was always my biggest encourager and my greatest fan.

ACKNOWLEDGEMENT

Thank you to my mum, who understands and encourages my love of poetry. Thank you to my late grandad, whom this book is dedicated to, who also supported my love of words and was always willing for me to share my poems with him (even when I was in a mental health hospital a few years ago).

Thank you to Manchester Metropolitan University Poetry Society for being such a friendly and creative space for sharing and critiquing poems (and for having a lot of fun)! Thank you also to Manchester Metropolitan University for their fabulous Third Term Project, Poetry for Wellbeing, which allowed me to nurture my passion for poetry and to share a poetry workshop with others. During the Third Term Project, I took part in a FutureLearn course created by Manchester Metropolitan University called 'How To Make A Poem.' It was discontinued in June 2022 but was an important source of inspiration for me, especially when it came to learning how to start the process of finding material for a poem and discovering techniques for editing poems.

Thank you to Turning Point, the charity that I currently work for, for giving me a platform to share my love of poetry when I ran a creative writing group in one of my previous roles as Peer Support Worker. Thank you also to Turning Point for the fabulous opportunity to have three of my poems published in a poetry book, 'Writing for Our Lives.' This book features work from people with experience of mental health issues or drug and alcohol problems. It is available to buy online, including on Amazon. This undoubtedly ignited a spark in me to publish more of my work.

PREFACE

I did not know whether to write a preface for my poetry book, so I will settle on giving some optional guidance. That is, I do hope that part of you resonates with the words in these poems and that they help you to make sense of your experiences in new ways. The interesting thing about the arts, including poetry, is that two people can look at the same thing and interpret it in completely different ways. I expect this to happen, and I wish for you that you will honour whatever you see in my poems.

Amidst the Madness

A space in time emerges -
amidst gritty mug stains,
and stinging flesh in water,
my steaming soul escaping,
through angular windows,
feelings collapsing like mud

A space in time emerges -
amongst life's admin,
piled high like Jenga,
soon to harshly topple,
so that my eyes gather dust,
and seep wet, just pain

A space in time emerges,
between the chaos surrounding,
the angered buzz of the TV,
the chatter biting my ears,
the hoarse roar of hedge-trimming

A space in time emerges,
so instead I shape a burrow,
away from disturbed peace,
savouring the comforting air,
breathing in the golden walls,
like they're luscious, bold pages,

and I perceive a neat phrase -

'You must write,'
            and I will.

A Soul-Filled Fight

I need a tonic for life,
a brave, rich syrup,
to bathe sores inside

I need a heart song.
Is it my true hope?
One of fresh trails?

Do I sip boldly,
at the nectar of life?
The joy of my smile?

Can I lighten the ache,
of my baffled veins?
Is the pen my sword?

I'll write with love,
when life's scarred hands,
smear my tender lungs

I'll write with force,
amongst raging wind,
choking my breath

Each day: a paradox,

a wise, bright phrase,
then black, stark grief

Each day: a challenge,
only *I* can hope:

the pen, nothing without *my* soul.

Bleeding Life

I purged,
so, I dared -
I bled onto
the sharpened pages.

And, like a blizzard,
my heart engulfed me,
it knew the metallic
blood of a thousand years -
the scent of pain.

But, my heart - it was
a valiant soldier,
it did not fear for its
thick, mottled loss.

For every stain,
was the chant
from a wise imagination -
a heart that knew no bounds,
that would make
triumphant *poetry*

out of the mess.

Flow

Ideas circle,
unwritten, like clammy
vapour on the tongue.
Until they're condensed,
then, a way appears?
But, at first,
heat scolds,
and silence echoes.

Warmth grows,
sliding down in sync
with love now.
Refined and pure, like
clear bubbles of hope,
that excite. It's
innocent labour:
mighty freedom.

This poem's a birth,
of a mind, now
not too stark or bold.
Balance considered,
once burning questions.
Now trickling,
in out, in out,
into hope.

A Life, Worn

My tender skin, bloodied
on rust, from a
weathered nail. I'm reminded
of my knees, also torn
- like they're battered sins.
The nail now seems the
culprit: acidic stench,
imposing, undressed.

My damp eyes,
view teeming piles.
Weathered receipts trigger
memories I wish to forget.
A rotten tale, formed
from tattered paper. Showing
a paid-for life: pain with freedom,
our indulgence and need.

Eager hands, stroke
something bouncy,
sparkling, bright – a ball.
Like childish dreams, smooth
and coloured, unspoiled.
I recall my youth –
a fountain of strength and

vitality – and being carefree.

Alert ears prick against
a digital watch, its
comforting pulse moving
with the rich currents of life.
Time is like a full harvest -
fruitful moments to
return to when we face
barren, harsh seasons.

Thus, my pockets bulge,
with strange peace,
with perplexed woes.
The physical evokes
many feelings –
from a life worn

and lived.

Well Lived?

Breathing into the cracks
of my throbbing back,
lugged forever -
a whole 30 years

Breathing into the cracks
of my pounding pupils,
fatigued from the strain -
of many years

And as I breathe,
I recall in haste -
the ache, the faults,
the battered stench
of endless surrender

Whispering to the cracks
of my teary,
suppressed palm -
of countless years

Whispering to the cracks
of my bleeding knees,
crushed and torn -
now matured in years

And as I whisper,
I shiver from the
agony and the toil,
of a path nailed forward
without safety, and ask -

All of this,
is the seasoned scar
of rich wisdom?

Of a life,
    well lived?

Questioning as I age,
there's both suffering
and blunt stupidity –
stretched through years

Questioning as I age,
I doubt wisdom,
hail the joyful child –
not wasting years

Is pain purposeful,
more than bleak exertion,
against the tide,
or the boldness
of withered eyes?

All of this,
is the confused scar
of tangled wisdom?

Of a life,
    well lived?

Grace

When we have given to life,
blood clogged with sweat,
hair knotted from strain,
face stained with concern,
soles toughened from life's race

It is then that we find solace,
in the perfect forms in nature,
soft passion of friends,
artful spark from poems,
bold portal in music

Oh, our senses awaken
to humanity,
needs,
longings,

grace.

Clean

From workdays dulled to a past thought,
I still rewind, to the patter of my feet,
composing a dragging tune. And,
my hand, caked in callouses, chafing,
chafing against screaming surfaces.
Ah, sweet labour – now and then.

Today, in all I do, that feeling
lingers. My life, untied, until corners
and crannies are revered - symbols of
time not wasted. I recall the steady slog
it took in hot, humid air. Now
used to polish a new practice.

Cleaning, a harsh meditation.
But change emerges, from a cloth
sticky with the stench of toxins.
I learnt not to flinch, despite my
pulse pounding from exertion.
And grew to respect. The work.

We could all glean more from
effort. Owning it as a symbol
of trust. Like an irate heart after
the gym. Only then, water tastes

sweet. Cleaning, a metaphor.
For learning, and peace.

Plea

My mind, my home,
were ashen stacks,
of stresses known,
of habits ungrown

There was much to do,
dull and pressing,
screeching the blues,
I was scared to lose

Respite so needed,
my joints craved care,
but people thought 'Needy,
why so conceited!'

Knuckles tainted,
blisters from strain,
my hobbies, fainted,
longed to be painted!

At sweetened air,
the cool relief,
I hollered 'Unfair, that
life will not share!'

But help escaped me
I begged to be still,
'Must I pay fees,
or bow to my knees?'

An answer emerges,
from rotten despair,
my insight urges,
hope freely surges

What I know now?
That I mustn't persist -
I make my heart drown,
here is the twist!

My Own Enemy

On seething wardrobes,
bulging piles were
starved of their hope,
dust cackled slyly
upon age-tinted books,
a pimpled witch
gave the orderly
its scathing looks

I grieved the peace
I had spat on
with pungent poison,
it cast dark spells,
upon the nooks
of my toppled calm…

My heavy heart
throbs with panic.

Now, I pray, urgently,
for raging flames,
to banish forever
this screeching plot,
it's my piercing shame,
blackened hope,

the dust as ugly,
as flaking, scolding ash

But, a voice upon
the evil mess,
now sings boldly:
'My friend, be gentle,
gentle's more imposing
than bleak magic –
softly dust off your
roaring self-hatred'

Feathers leaping,
objects glimmer,
beam like dragonflies,
the air dances,
shines away
the now cowered spell...

I am my own fairy –
as I was my own witch.

The Paradox of Pain

My flesh pulsed as I was bolted below,
to a chair spiked with roughened gravel,
'Life's fool and cursed' spat the air,
its screeching gusts a muddled siren

I was bitten with scorching poison,
as pain rattled through my veins,
burnt features thrashed onto a mirror -
I lurched and choked on the ground

Self-hatred was the sinful culprit,
driving beastly bulges in my limbs -
and forming scars, like bleeding
bruises from cowered hearts' foes

I confronted myself from another angle,
and chains retired like peaceful mud,
ready to be welcomed home again,
into the nourished soil below

Perception now the hopeful cure,
renewing each ugly atom,
and I will bow down in mercy:

no easy freedom *without* pain.

A Journey from God

God, do I feel growth?
Can I sense it through
my longing heart?
Will it cleanse my blood?

My kin, I have but a map,
serrated here and there
with your earnt blood -
an agonised touch

God, can I see growth?
As a tapestry, bold
and vivid as a life
truly trod?

My child, the edges
blend and merge -
as the path diverts,
and can be greyish mud

God, can I smell growth?
Like a fresh flower
waking my nostrils
with clear love?

My friend, rarely has

the way been lined
with sweet scent -
it can trigger deep loss

God, can I taste growth?
Does it stand softly
on my dancing,
renewed tongue?

My soul, I must think,
that you are missing
the crux of the matter -
the shocking truth

But, God, can I hear growth?
Is it really not a birdsong?
Or a peaceful chant
soothing my ears?

Here, now - come
upon my shoulder
and rest in my name,
the truth I have not spoken...

That a journey
forged with growth
it is so tough...
but that's the real
                beauty-full.

Earth School*

In the solace of outstretched palms,
beckoning a steadfast sun
that tickles my sinews and nerves -
I still thirst for a new world

In my potent reflections,
I see myself in another's skin,
their soft, dainty fingers -
but raging against a thousand wrongs

In the temple of my heart,
I can compose a rhythm
to enthrone comforting thoughts -
but I have yet to embrace the BBC News

In all the giving and taking,
burdened worries and soft joy,
insight and rough confusion,
I have yet to welcome the paradox...

When in pleasure I must not reject pain,
in all the pain I should not ignore smiles,
to mingle my past and present
feelings is not a paradox …

But the *one* answer in an uncertain

Earth School*.

---

*Earth School is a concept found in the work of the spiritual teacher, Gary Zukav (seatofthesoul.com).

Answering the Call

When I deny feelings,
I armour up with concrete
lips and a concrete lung,
lifeless on my tongue,
when I should be
feeding a healthy pulse

When I pretend that I am
not as deep as the earth's core,
I live in my shell out at sea,
oblivious to the call
of vast warmth, that tingles
at my squashed feet

When I please others, who
am I, but a clammy belt
suffocating bright joy?
I wear a 'one size fits all' -
but ignore the rhythmic
call of *my* life

When I only dance on one leg,
I am but a smattering of my
real truth - a deep panic
rumbles upon my strangled throat,

numbness invades my blood

And there I wish for the
night or the dawn *alone*,
when *every* moment is a gift.
This, a choice so profound that
my pain begins to fade –
hollering for the new...

And despite all else,
an insight beckons,
and it beckons - amongst
the backdrop of my
(cleansing) thirst,
amongst a backdrop of
(comforting) hope

And that's when I know -
I am more than a gabble
of mumbling thoughts
and other's desires.
I am a deep flow, and I
answer that call...

My tattered armour -
the *gateway* to change,
but so unneeded now.

The Gateway

By the door, we hover,
one foot in the dirt,
one in the coaxing waves

Do we stay trodden,
or gear up and float?

Do we breathe in clean air,
does it slip seamlessly,
through our lungs?

Or do we feel torn,
by a twanging thorn,
on the backdrop of stone?

Can the sea drive us on,
challenge our fears,
whisper softly through the sky?

Can the dirt encase us,
collapse upon our skin,
at a heightened pelt?

Do we really choose,
are we engulfed by life -

Lord, can we choose?

*My friend, you can
let the world decide,
but you sense a need -
why not accept that call?*

Non-Sense?

You have a song to teach,
before your padded feet,
sink in remorse, towards
rotten, stained glue

You have a song to teach,
one strong enough to leap,
with a pretty tweet,
as purple as you know

You will sing it,
when you loosen your
tangled teeth, and the
scent of metal concern

You will sing it, when
children hop in the sky,
against the backdrop,
of a laughing sun

You will perceive, that
it's beyond the bellow,
of a studded horse,
aching from the downpour

You will perceive, that
it's the saint,
who warms the ice,
with caramel toes

You will know, in your
joy and your fading pain,
a world beyond
sensible words -
towards your *imaginings*:

your soul.

The Shades of Difference

Being different is purple,
poised royalty, all gold,
it's pouncing on your toes,
so certain and free

Being different is red,
the rich depth of life,
your electric giving,
never dampened by night

Being different is black,
daggers have punctured
your hunched, lonely chest,
bent double with aches

Being different is brown,
full of confused cells,
icy to the touch,
rabbles of weak thoughts

Difference is joy and pain,
an array of events.

It's standing up bold,
then fading to grey.

Beyond the City Buzz

Moulded to the soft seat,
you were a silent statue,
still against the air,
viewing the shiny track

Men sported sleek suits,
contented, as though in pjs,
clasped briefcases boldly,
those angular boxes

They marched off, like
horses ready for dressage,
phone calls flowed to and fro,
like a chattering radio

Now, you sit, and wait.
The slick scene confusing,
tangling your nerves -
'Will I get to where *I* belong?'

The city melts to a huddle,
to a mumble in your ear,
the sun, a silent giggle,
the day dawns on you

Train groans to a halt,
you exit with a relieved sigh,
to an ever-growing meadow,
sweet as summer cordial

The city buzz is swallowed,
to the depths of your throat,
this is where you belong,
where all you need to do

- is to *observe*.

Alone

You wake up, get up,
another day, different day,
belt up, hoist up,
sips, sweet and warm,
fresh dawn -
what now for?

Step out, stiffen up,
ahead a cute couple,
their bright cheeks,
bitter thoughts, then
to yourself,
'Don't feel alone,
God says grow,
this sign can go?'

Enter work,
head up, chin up,
cracks barely slip,
others laugh,
normal show, your face,
creased now, heated
yet cold,
should you worry,
perhaps not so?

End of day,
meek smile, shy voice,
pet a pleased dog,
go home, empty,
grin melts, dark
scene - solo seat.

Shoulders slide,
face falls,
radio on,
a fizz, a bellow,
endless sobs -
your life, robbed.

Radio on, once more,
then strangely so,
a machine, the one that plays,
soft songs, real songs - calling
'Don't stand alone.'

Purposeful Encounters

A touch in the depths of winter,
purposeful encounters,
strengthened winks,
happiness never so sweet,
wisdom pulsating through skin,
the aroma of rich coffee,
smooth across my lips

A coffee shop in the morning,
is a welcomed gift,
that freely glides open,
set amongst strangers,
bright, unexpected friends,
at first, distant
– yet not separate

The morning's a protected bud,
has survived the frosty night,
breaks apart difference,
I see with glittering eyes anew,
our shared humanity,
cast upon shadows -
and perceive beyond our cloaks.

Covid Was Our World

When all this is over, we'll
enter cafes full of human stories,
lit by rich caramel scents,
both soothing our minds

When all this is over, we'll take off
barriers choking our breath,
eyes will shimmer like mirrors,
reflecting hope onto life

When all this is over, we'll
embrace each other gladly,
kindness healing open wounds,
touch lighting the path

But for now, we sense the
need for a warm whisper,
to refresh our chapped lips,
instead – we know distance

But for now, we see
that the rich cologne of love,
in a bustling room of souls,
is sadly not yet ours to give

But for now, here's the truth,
misery is stomped out gladly,
with a stroll in dancing leaves,
or a sweet phone call,

portal to *another* world…
yet to return.